Do You Like Keeping Up with Fashion?

Diane Lindsey Reeves

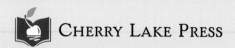

CHERRY LAKE PRESS

Published in the United States of America by Cherry Lake Publishing Group
Ann Arbor, Michigan
www.cherrylakepublishing.com

Reading Adviser: Beth Walker Gambro, MS, Ed., Reading Consultant, Yorkville, IL

Photo Credits: cover: © AnnaStills/Shutterstock; page 5: © Ursula Page/Shutterstock; page 6: © ESB Professional/
Shutterstock; page 7: © Pixel-Shot/Shutterstock; page 8: © Krakenimages.com/Shutterstock; page 9: © Odua Images/
Shutterstock; page 10: © Andre Roque Almeida/Shutterstock; page 11: © maratr/Shutterstock; page 12: © Jacob
Lund/Shutterstock; page 13: © Yaoinlove/Shutterstock; page 14: © Joa Souza/Shutterstock; page 15: © Monkey
Business Images/Shutterstock; page 16: © wavebreakmedia/Shutterstock; page 17: © Rawpixel.com/Shutterstock;
page 18: © adriaticfoto/Shutterstock; page 19: © AS photostudio/Shutterstock; page 20: © FashionStock.com/
Shutterstock; page 21: © Rad K/Shutterstock; page 22: © suprabhat/Shutterstock; page 23: © Victoria Lipov/
Shutterstock; page 24: © UfaBizPhoto/Shutterstock; pages 25, 31: © SeventyFour/Shutterstock; page 26: © yurakrasil/
Shutterstock; page 27: © BearFotos/Shutterstock; page 30: © Olena Yakobchuk/Shutterstock

Cherry Lake Press is an imprint of Cherry Lake Publishing Group.

Library of Congress Cataloging-in-Publication Data

Names: Reeves, Diane Lindsey, 1959- author.
Title: Do you like keeping up with fashion? / Diane Lindsey Reeves.
Description: Ann Arbor, Michigan : Cherry Lake Publishing, [2023] | Series: Career clues for kids | Includes
    bibliographical references and index. | Audience: Grades 4-6
Summary: "Do you like putting outfits together or starting fashion trends? That might be a potential clue to your
    future career! This book explores what a career in fashion might look like. Readers will discover how their interests
    can lead to a lifelong future career. Aligned to curriculum standards and 21st Century Skills, Career Clues for
    Kids prepares readers for a successful future. Includes table of contents, glossary, index, sidebars, and author
    biographies"— Provided by publisher.
Identifiers: LCCN 2022039248 | ISBN 9781668919477 (hardcover) | ISBN 9781668920497 (paperback) |
    ISBN 9781668921821 (ebook) | ISBN 9781668923153 (pdf)
Subjects: LCSH: Fashion—Vocational guidance—Juvenile literature. | Clothing trade—Vocational guidance—
    Juvenile literature.
Classification: LCC TT507 .R384 2023 | DDC 746.9/2023—dc23/eng/20220826
LC record available at https://lccn.loc.gov/2022039248

Cherry Lake Publishing Group would like to acknowledge the work of the Partnership for 21st Century Learning,
a Network of Battelle for Kids. Please visit *http://www.battelleforkids.org/networks/p21* for more information.

Printed in the United States of America
Corporate Graphics

Diane Lindsey Reeves likes to write books that help students figure out what they want
to be when they grow up. She mostly lives in Washington, D.C., but spends as much time
as she can in North Carolina and South Carolina with her grandkids.

CONTENTS

Find a Fashionable Career

Figuring out what you want to be when you grow up can be tricky. There are so many choices! How are you supposed to know which one to pick? Here's an idea... follow the clues!

The fact that you are reading a book called *Do You Like Keeping Up with Fashion?* is your first clue. It suggests that you might be a **fashionista**. True? If so, start looking at different careers where you can style your way into a cool future!

Your **interests** say a lot about who you are and what makes you tick. What do you like doing best?

Abilities are things that you are naturally good at doing. Another word for ability is talent. Everyone has natural talents and abilities. Some are more obvious than others. What are you really good at doing?

Curiosity offers up other career clues. To succeed in any career, you must learn what it takes to do that job. You may have to go to college or trade school. It may take gaining new skills and getting experience. Curiosity about a subject keeps you at it until you learn what you need to know. What do you want to know more about?

Interests. Abilities. Curiosity. These clues can help you find a career that's right for you.

FIND THE CLUES!

Each chapter includes several clues about careers you might enjoy.

INTERESTS: **What do you like doing?**

ABILITIES: **What are you good at doing?**

CURIOSITY: **What do you want to learn more about?**

Are You a Future Fashionista?

WOULD YOU ENJOY...

Selling cute outfits in a store? (see page 8)

Creating costumes for a Broadway play? (see page 10)

Setting up a shop online? (see page 12)

Going on a super-duper shopping binge? (see page 14)

Designing the latest fashions? (see page 16)

Strutting your stuff in a fashion show? (see page 18)

Blogging about the latest looks? (see page 20)

Filling your favorite store with fashionable brands?
(see page 22)

Figuring out how clothes are made? (see page 24)

Helping customers shop till they drop? (see page 26)

READ ON FOR
MORE CLUES ABOUT
FASHIONABLE
CAREERS!

Boutique Manager

A person who manages a small shop that sells fashionable clothes, shoes, or jewelry.

Boutiques sell certain types of products for certain types of **customers**. Maybe it's baby clothes to new parents or high-end designer clothes to women with plenty of money to spend. Bring on the latest jeans and cool T-shirts for tweens! These stores have a **vibe** that appeals to its intended target market. Fresh flowers and water bottles for the ladies. Pop music and fun colors for the tweens. Boutique managers set the tone and serve the customers. Boutique managers need business skills to run and market their stores. It helps when they are really into the products they sell.

CLUES!

INTEREST: Shopping in fun local stores

ABILITY: Putting together outfits other people notice

CURIOSITY: The business side of fashion

INVESTIGATE!

NOW: Check out different vibes at local boutiques.

LATER: Get retail sales experience and management training.

Costume Designer

A person who designs costumes for a film, stage production, or TV show.

Can you imagine putting together complete wardrobes for everyone in your class? That's pretty much what costume designers do for a cast of actors. Each character has their own look. Each occasion has its own style. Costume designers do three jobs in one. They are part fashion designer, part history researcher, and part **tailor**. Costumes set the stage and clue viewers in about what's going on. Is it a futuristic film about life on Mars? Or ancient Vikings on the warpath? Maybe it's kids in a TV comedy. The clothes tell the story and make things seem real.

CLUES!

INTEREST: Paying more attention to what actors wear than what they say

ABILITY: Putting together the best Halloween costumes

CURIOSITY: The history of fashion

INVESTIGATE!

NOW: Learn how to sew.

LATER: Earn a college degree in fashion design, theater design, or art history.

E-Commerce Manager

A person who manages an online store.

It used to be that you went to a shopping mall to buy new clothes. You can still do that. You can also shop at any store you can imagine on your home computer. All it takes is a few clicks and a credit card—used only with permission! **E-commerce** managers run these online stores. They use technology to set up the online store. They use fashion savvy to fill it with products customers want to buy. Their marketing know-how drives traffic to the website. Cha-ching! That sound says they are doing a good job.

CLUES!

INTEREST: Checking out your favorite online stores

ABILITY: Using your laptop and smartphone like a boss

CURIOSITY: How technology makes life better

INVESTIGATE!

NOW: Compare a mall store with its online store.

LATER: Earn a college degree in business or marketing.

Fashion Buyer

A person who makes purchasing decisions for a clothing retailer.

Do you like to shop till you drop? Fashion buyers do. Only they don't shop to fill their own closets. They shop to fill entire stores! The job gives them a front-row seat to the latest looks at fashion shows and designer showrooms. Every season brings new chances to discover new fashion must-haves from fashion brands and manufacturers. "What styles will people buy?" is a big question. Fashion buyers answer this question with data on sales, celebrity fashion news, and their own fashion sense. Sometimes fashion buyers follow fashion trends. Sometimes they create their own!

CLUES!

INTEREST: Staying one step ahead of the latest styles

ABILITY: Creating new looks with old outfits

CURIOSITY: How fashion trends catch on

INVESTIGATE!

NOW: Make a list of all the current fashion must-haves.

LATER: Earn a college degree in fashion merchandising.

Fashion Designer

A person who creates original clothing, accessories, and footwear.

The latest fashion trends start in the imagination of fashion designers. The best-known fashion designers design high-end looks for big fashion shows in New York City, Paris, and other fashion hubs. Most fashion designers create fun new looks that people wear every day. They design everything from dresses and jeans to pj's and socks. They design clothes for men, women, children, and even babies. The work requires a creative streak and a love of color. Fashion designers sketch out and sew samples of their best ideas. You'll find them working for all of your favorite brands and stores.

CLUES!

INTEREST: Reading fashion magazines

ABILITY: Sketching ideas for new outfits

CURIOSITY: The history of fashion

INVESTIGATE!

NOW: Keep tabs on fashion trends at your school.

LATER: Earn a college degree in fashion design or merchandising.

Fashion Model

A person who poses to display clothing on stage or in photos.

Fashion models show off clothes from designers and fashion brands. They pose for photos that appear in magazines, commercials, and store catalogs. Big-name models also walk the runways of famous fashion shows around the world. The clothes they wear are super expensive and set the tone for each fashion season. Catalog models wear clothes with appeal for everyday life. The clothes they wear can be sporty and fun, all business, or ready to party. They make clothes look so good that other people want to buy them. Modeling can be glamorous, but it is hard work, too!

CLUES!

INTEREST: Thumbing through catalogs or scrolling through websites from your favorite stores

ABILITY: Knowing different ways to pose in photos and selfies

CURIOSITY: How to create a modeling portfolio

INVESTIGATE!

NOW: Get involved in school fashion shows.

LATER: Attend a **reputable** modeling school and connect with a solid talent agency.

Fashion Writer

A journalist or blogger who writes about fashion.

Love fashion and love to write? How about a career as a fashion writer? Fashion writers write for magazines, newspapers, websites, and TV shows. One day they may be researching a story about fashion trends or interviewing a famous fashion designer. Another day it's reporting all the juicy details of a major fashion show. Some fashion writers have their own blogs and promote styles from different designers. They are known as influencers when lots of fans follow their posts. Coming up with story ideas is a big part of the job. Like other writers, the key is finding your own voice.

CLUES!

INTEREST: Fashion magazines and blogs

ABILITY: Writing things people like to read

CURIOSITY: How to be a fashion influencer

INVESTIGATE!

NOW: Write stories about your favorite fashions.

LATER: Earn a college degree in journalism or English.

Merchandiser

A person who designs and creates attractive visual displays at retail stores.

A merchandiser's job is to promote products and increase sales. They do this in lots of fun ways. It could be a window display that makes people stop and look. It could be a beautifully dressed **mannequin** that makes people say, "I want that outfit!" It could be signs advertising a big sale. Merchandisers may even plan the layout for an entire store to make it easy to find the good stuff. They use technology to keep track of hot products and duds. This data guides choices about sales and displays. Always keep that merch moving!

CLUES!

INTERESTS: Checking out window displays at your favorite stores

ABILITIES: Selling stuff for school sales

CURIOSITY: What fashion marketing is all about

INVESTIGATE!

NOW: Get involved in your school's pep club to help "sell" sports events.

LATER: Earn at least a 2-year college degree in fashion merchandising.

Patternmaker

A person who creates plans or diagrams used as a guide in making clothes.

Lots of people have never heard of patternmakers. But if you are wearing clothes that fit, it's because a patternmaker did a good job. Clothes are made by sewing pieces of material together in a certain way. Patternmakers figure out the best way to put each item together. They create "blueprints" or patterns that manufacturers use to make an item in all different sizes. It takes a mix of math skills and fashion know-how to get the measurements right. Patternmakers are a link between a fashion designer's ideas and a finished product.

CLUES!

INTEREST: Sewing your own clothes

ABILITY: Following patterns to make an outfit

CURIOSITY: How clothes are mass-produced

INVESTIGATE!

NOW: Take a sewing class.

LATER: Get training in fashion production.

Personal Shopper

A person who helps people choose clothes to buy or buys clothes for them.

Ready for a shopping marathon? Personal shoppers are professional shoppers who help clients look their best. They get to know each client's personal style and find clothes and accessories to build their wardrobes. They are experts in knowing what styles work for different body types. They match outfits to fit each client's lifestyle. The trick is to understand the client's taste so well that they choose nicer clothes than the client would choose for themself! Personal shoppers are also called wardrobe consultants or personal stylists. They either work for department stores or have their own businesses.

CLUES!

INTERESTS: Shopping in all kinds of stores

ABILITIES: Helping friends pick out outfits for school events

CURIOSITY: How people like to dress

INVESTIGATE!

NOW: Make a scrapbook with pictures of your favorite fashion looks.

LATER: Get experience working in fashion retail stores.

Fashion Workshop

Keep investigating those career clues until you find a career that's right for you! Here are more ways to explore.

Join a Club

Find out if your school has a Family, Career, and Community Leaders of America club (https://fcclainc.org) and get involved.

Talk to People with Interesting Careers

Ask your teacher or parent to help you connect with someone who has a career like the one you want. Be ready to ask lots of questions!

Volunteer

Help organize a clothing or coat drive for needy families at your school or place of worship.

Enjoy Career Day

School career days can be a great way to find out more about different careers. Make the most of this opportunity.

Explore Online

With adult supervision, use your favorite search engine to look online for information about careers you are interested in.

Participate in Take Your Daughters and Sons to Work Day

Every year on the fourth Thursday of April, kids all over the world go to work with their parents or other trusted adults to find out what the world of work is really like.

Find out more at: https://daughtersandsonstowork.org

Resources

Boutique Manager
Buzzfeed: 21 Places to Buy Tweens Their New Favorite Clothes
https://www.buzzfeed.com/ryleejohnston/best-clothing-stores-for-tweens

Costume Designer
Metropolitan Museum of Art: The Costume Institute
https://www.metmuseum.org/about-the-met/collection-areas/the-costume-institute

e-Commerce Manager
Scratch
https://scratch.mit.edu

Fashion Buyer
YouTube: What I Do as a Fashion Buyer
https://www.youtube.com/watch?v=MQlfiJV6SRk

Fashion Designer
Quigley, Kerri. *Fashion Design for Kids.* Emeryville, CA: Rockridge Press, 2021.

Fashion Model
New York Fashion Week
https://nyfw.com/home

Fashion Writer
Stylecraze: 15 Best Fashion Bloggers
https://www.stylecraze.com/articles/best-fashion-blogs

Patternmaker
YouTube: Fabric and Apparel Patternmaker
https://www.youtube.com/watch?v=KP_EF4OMpGQ

Personal Shopper
Bravo: 10 Things Personal Shoppers Know about Shopping
https://www.bravotv.com/blogs/10-secrets-personal-shoppers-know-about-shopping

Merchandiser
Shopify: What is Visual Merchandising?
https://www.shopify.com/retail/visual-merchandising

Glossary

abilities (uh-BIH-luh-teez) natural talents or acquired skills

boutique (boo-TEEK) small shop that sells fashionable clothing

curiosity (kyur-ee-AH-suh-tee) strong desire to know or learn about something

customers (KUH-stuh-muhrs) people who buy goods or services

e-commerce (EE-kah-muhrs) process of buying or selling goods online

fashionista (fah-shuh-NEE-stuh) devoted follower of fashion

influencers (IN-floo-uhn-suhrs) people who promote products or services through social media

interests (IN-tuh-ruhsts) things or activities that a person enjoys or is concerned about

mannequin (MAH-nih-kuhn) human-like form used to display clothes in a store

tailor (TAY-luhr) person who sews or alters clothes to fit people

vibe (VYB) mood or character of a place

Index